Kawaii

CUPCAKES

COLORING BOOK

Cute Coloring Books for Adults

COLOR TEST PAGE

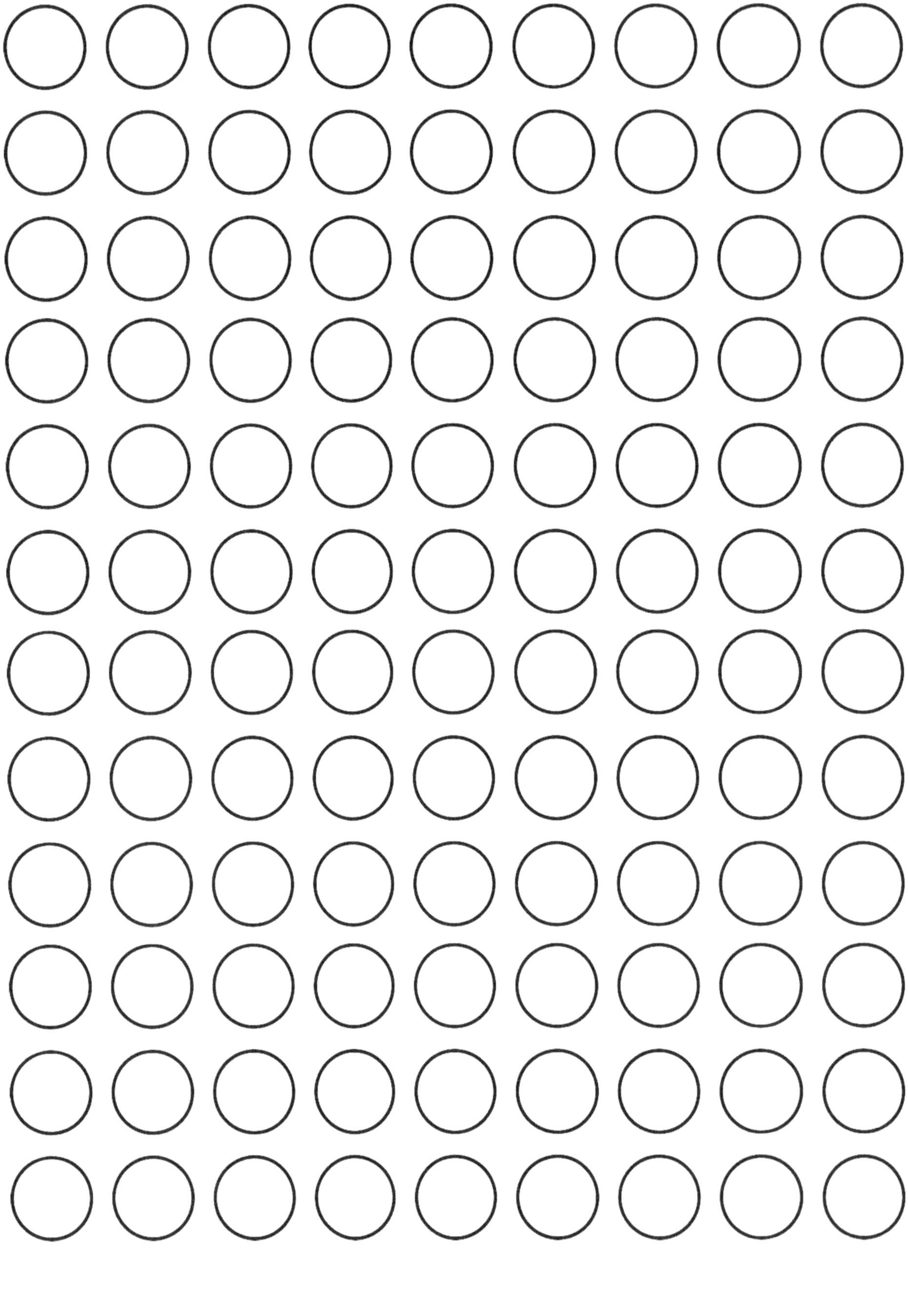

COLOR TEST PAGE

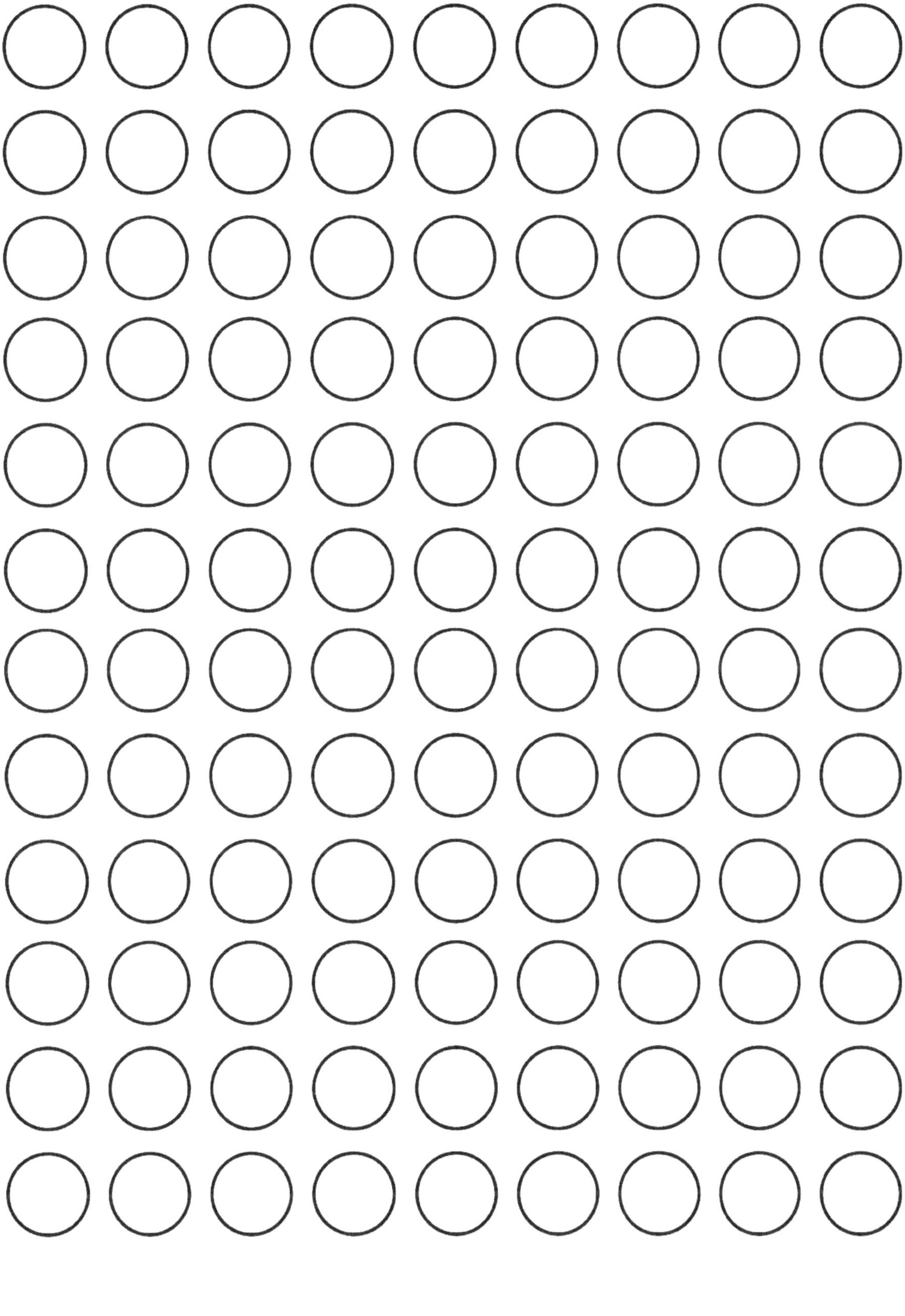

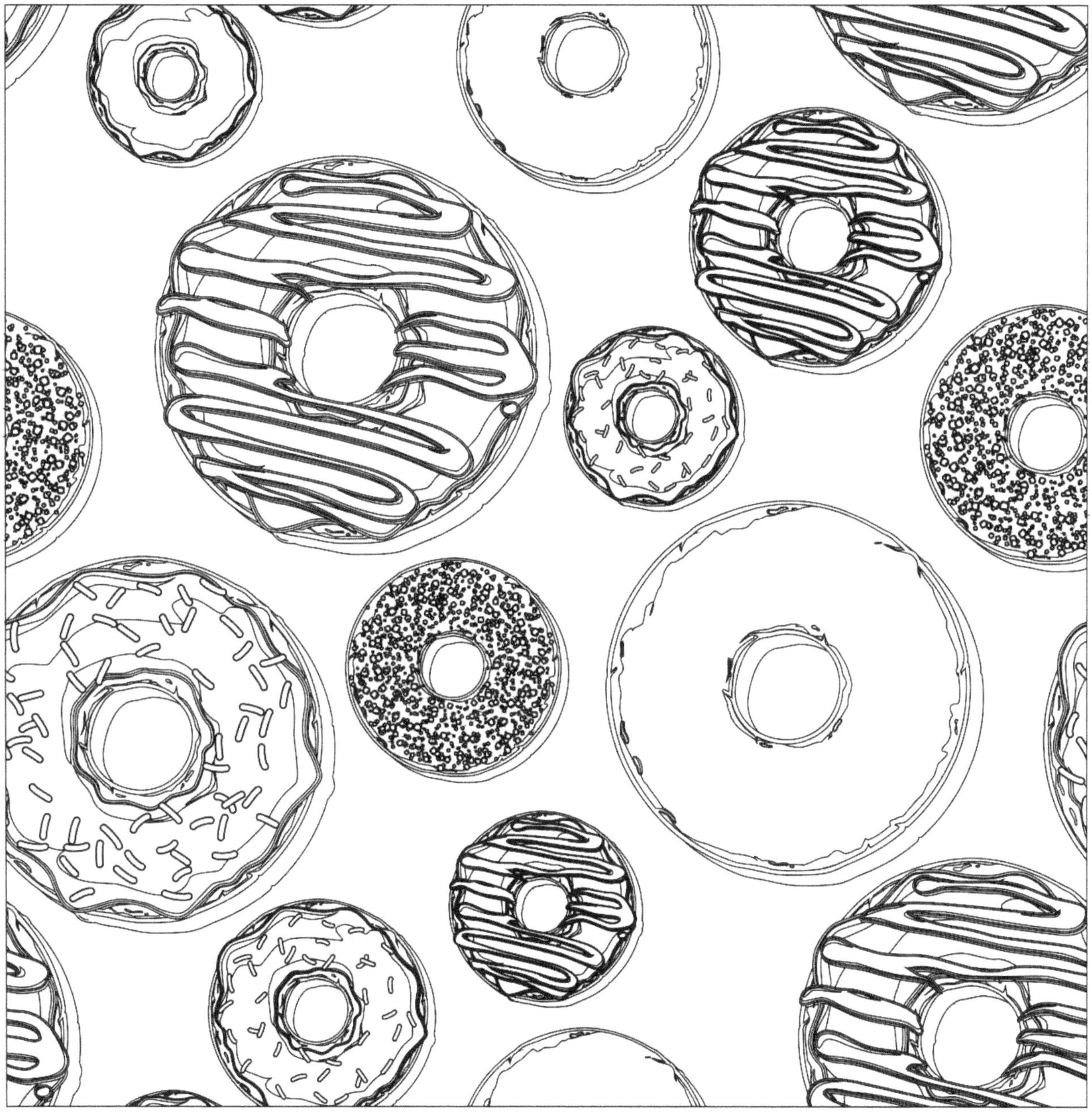

WELCOME

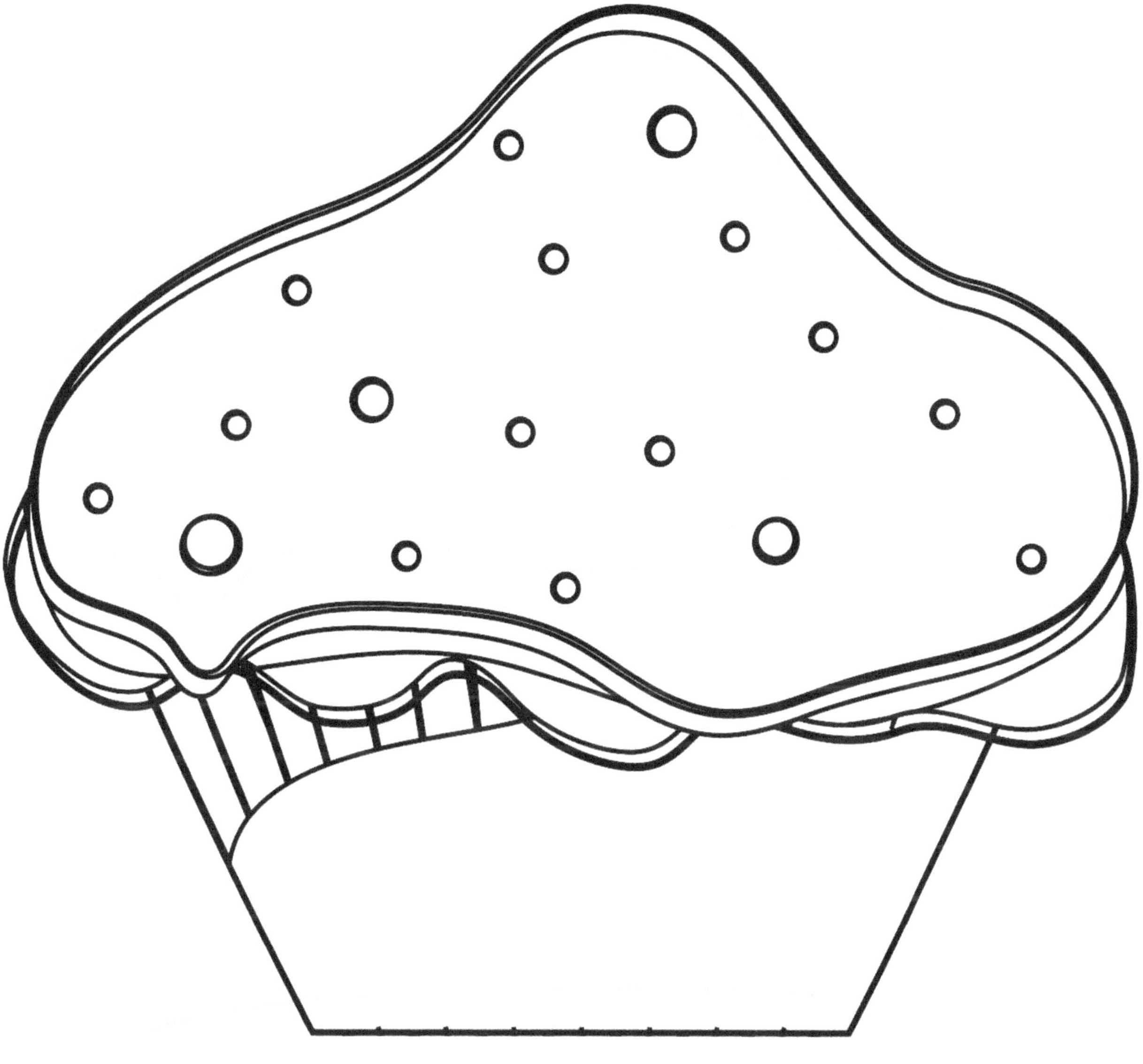

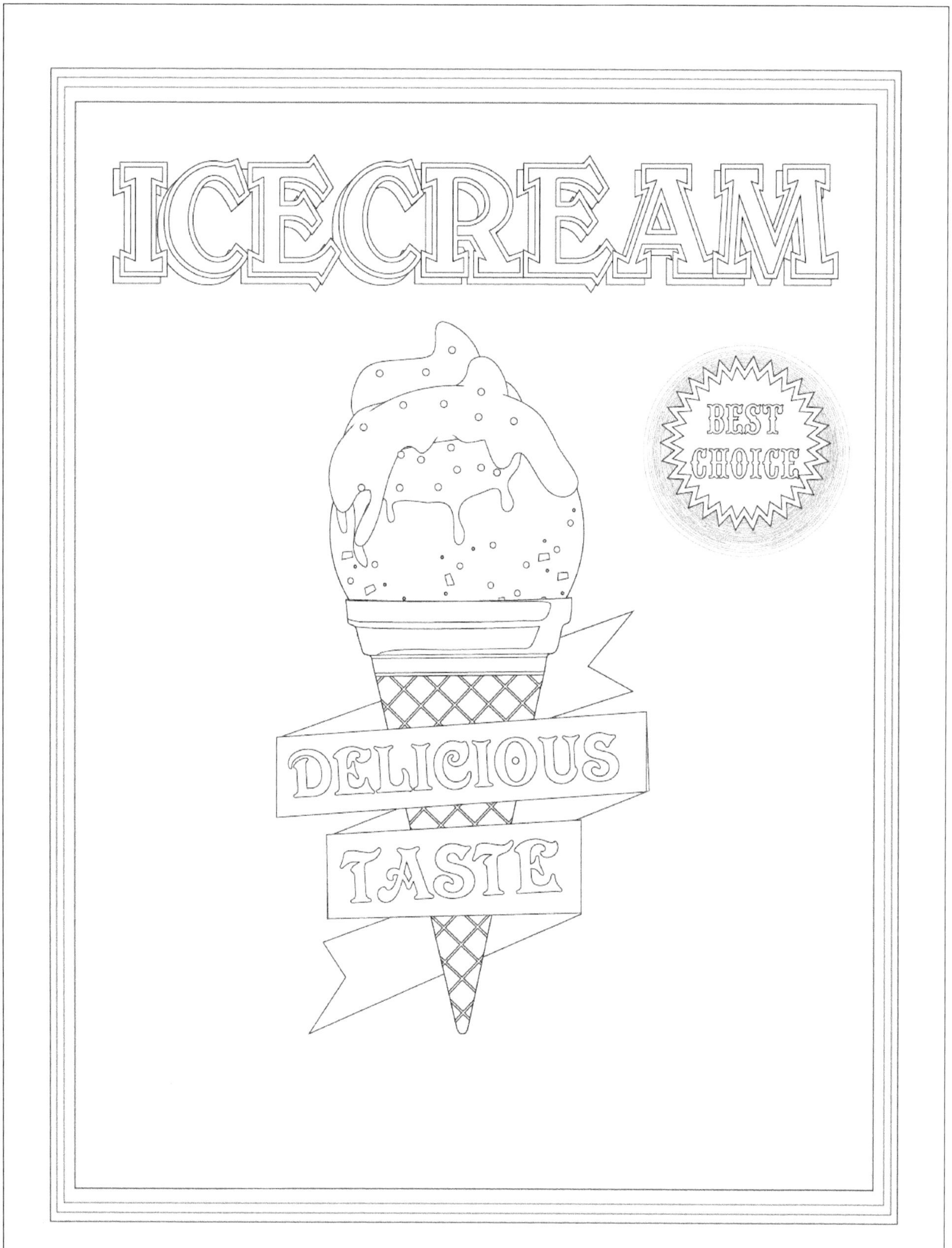
ICECREAM
BEST CHOICE
DELICIOUS
TASTE

Great taste every time

5$

MADE WITH LOVE

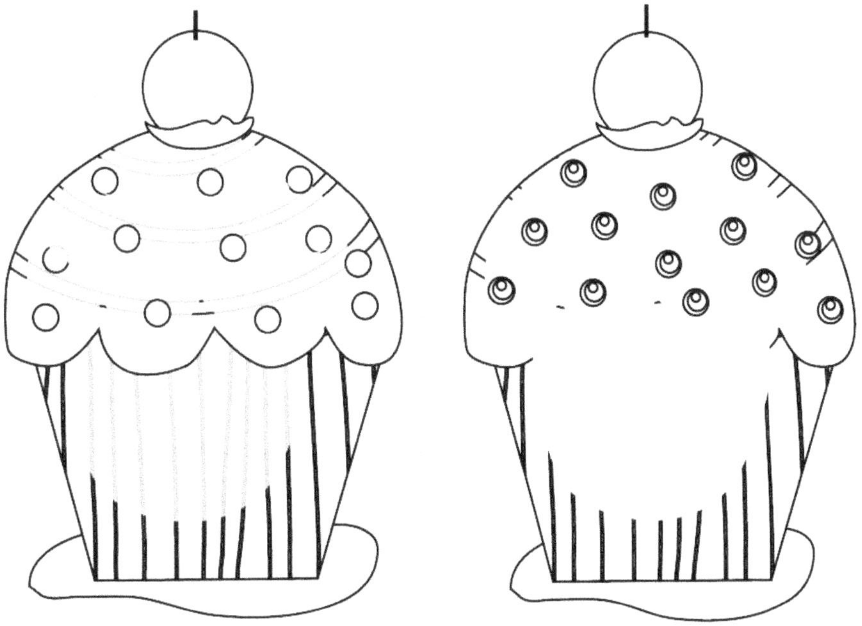

ICE CREAM
Delicious
Always
FRESH
BEST IN TOWN
BU NOW

Tea

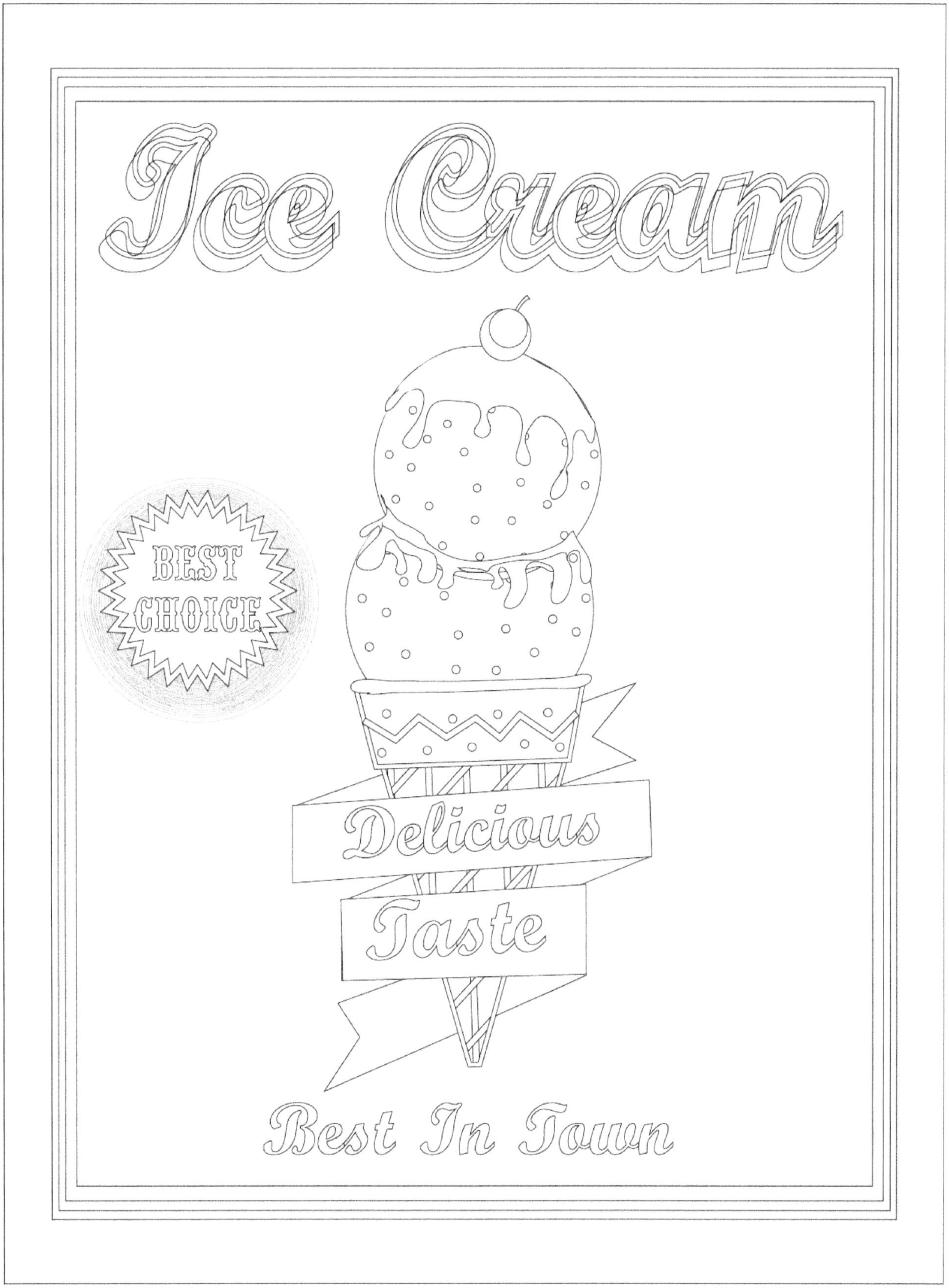
Ice Cream
BEST
CHOICE
Delicious
Taste
Best In Town

Tea

www.ingramcontent.com/pod-product-compliance
Lightning Source LLC
Chambersburg PA
CBHW080603190526
45169CB00007B/2864
* 9 7 8 1 5 3 5 2 2 9 8 6 9 *